Reading for TODAY

Workbook Five

PROGRAM AUTHORS

Linda Ward Beech • **Tara McCarthy**

PROGRAM CONSULTANTS

Myra K. Baum
Office of Adult and
    Continuing Education
Brooklyn, New York

Francis J. Feltman, Jr.
Racine Youth Offender
    Correctional Facility
Racine, Wisconsin

Mary Ann Guilliams
Gary Job Corps
San Marcos, Texas

Julie Jacobs
Inmate Literacy Project
Santa Clara County Library
Milpitas, California

Maxine L. McCormick
Workforce Education
Orange County Public Schools
Orlando, Florida

Sandra S. Owens
Laurens County Literacy Council
Laurens, South Carolina

STECK-VAUGHN
ELEMENTARY · SECONDARY · ADULT · LIBRARY

A Harcourt Company

www.steck-vaughn.com

Acknowledgments

STAFF CREDITS

Executive Editor: Ellen Northcutt

Senior Editor: Donna Townsend

Supervising Designer: Pamela Heaney

Designer: Jessica Bristow

ILLUSTRATION CREDITS: Scott Bieser, Joan Pilch

ISBN 0-7398-2957-2

Printed in the United State of America

9 10 11 12 13 14 15 1421 14 13 12 11

4500293714

Contents

To the Instructor

The *Reading for Today* workbooks are designed to accompany the new structure of the *Reading for Today* student books. Books 1–6 have corresponding workbooks that follow the same format in:

- controlled vocabulary
- reading level
- phonics and word-building skills
- sight vocabulary
- writing and comprehension skills

Student Book ➡️	Workbook
UNIT CONTENTS	**UNIT CONTENTS**
• Discussion	• Discussion
• Sight words	• Reading practice
• Phonics skills	• Phonics generalizations
• Writing skills	• Writing applications
• Reading selection	• Extended reading selection
• Comprehension questions	• Comprehension questions
• Life-coping skills	• Writing practice

The chart shows how a typical unit in a *Reading for Today* workbook serves as a follow-up for its corresponding unit in a *Reading for Today* student book.

Students who use the *Reading for Today* workbooks, however, do not simply review, practice, and reinforce sight words, phonics, and writing skills. Students also extend their learning. They read additional adult-related stories that are written with the controlled vocabulary that puts the reading within their grasp. Students discuss what they bring of their own experience to the reading selections by responding to purpose-setting questions, thus sharpening their thinking and discussion skills. And students write, both to demonstrate comprehension and to respond in their own way to the reading selections.

Teaching Suggestions

Each unit in the *Reading for Today* workbooks follows the pattern outlined below.

Reading and Discussing Page 3

Objectives: To help the student see the connection between reading and speaking. To improve comprehension through discussion.

Teaching Steps:

A. Read the question or questions. Encourage the learner to talk about the question. Discussing the question will help the student get ready to read the story that follows.

B. Help the student read the story. Remember to praise the learner's efforts.

C. Talk about the story. Help the student answer the discussion question that follows the story. Reread the story if necessary.

Review Words   Page 4

Objective: To review the sight words introduced in previous units.

Teaching Steps: Be sure the student understands the directions for each exercise. Have students check their answers by referring to the Answer Key at the back of the book.

Sight Words   Page 5

Objectives: To review the sight words learned in the corresponding student book unit. To practice reading word groups or phrases rather than individual words.

Teaching Steps:

A. Help the student read and reread each phrase until each one is smooth and natural. Move your hand or a pencil in an arc under each phrase as the learner reads, to help "push" the reader toward fluency. Praise the learner's success.

B. Help the student fill in the blanks correctly.

C. Practice reading the entire story for fluency. Rereading the story after practicing the phrasing will give the learner a sense of success.

Phonics Practice   Pages 6 and 7

Objective: To review and reinforce the phonics skills taught in the student book.

Teaching Steps: Be sure the learner understands the directions for each exercise. Have students check their answers by referring to the Answer Key at the back of the book.

Writing Skills   Page 8

Objective: To review and reinforce the writing skills taught in the student book.

Teaching Steps: Help the learner understand the directions for each exercise. Have students check their answers by referring to the Answer Key at the back of the book.

Comprehension   Page 9

Objectives: To read the conclusion of the story and answer comprehension questions in writing.

Teaching Steps:

A. Have the student read the story.

B. Have the student write the answers to the questions. The following hints will help the learner succeed.
   1. The answer to the question may often be found stated directly in the story.
   2. Rereading the story after reading a question may make it easier to answer the question.
   3. Some questions can be answered by turning the question into a statement and completing the statement with the answer from the story.

From Reading to Writing   Page 10

Objectives: To give students an opportunity to write about their own lives or life experiences. To reinforce reading by writing something for someone else to read.

Teaching Steps:

A. Encourage the learner to get as many ideas or thoughts on paper as possible. Praise any legitimate attempts to write. Try for more clarity only as your student gains confidence in writing.

B. When your student finishes writing, you may wish to go back over the writing and follow the suggestions in Part B of each writing page.

READING AND DISCUSSING

A. Talk about it.

How do different colors make you feel?

B. Read the story.

The Colors of a Sunset

"Hi! I'm home," April said as she walked into her apartment. She was beat, but that was OK. April loved her job. She worked as a painter for Mr. Baker, and she learned something new every day.

As she went to get cleaned up, her son Manny gave her a big hug. "So, what colors did people like today?" he asked. Manny and his brother Hector asked this a lot because April always had a good tale to tell. It seemed that people having their home or business painted thought a lot about color. Anything was possible when it came to how different colors made people feel.

April laughed. "Well, today I went to see the owner of Spark's Grill," she said. "You know, that's the new grill in the building on First Street."

"Right," said Manny, "I pass it every day. Let's see . . . a new grill. I bet she wants something dark on the walls. Eating places like grills are always painted in dark colors."

"Think again!" said April. "Mrs. York has something different in mind. She's decided to paint her business the colors of a sunset. Do you know why? She says it's because sunset is when people come in to eat and drink, at the end of the day when the sun is going down. She wants colors like blue, pink, gold, and maybe a bit of red."

"I like the feeling of that," said Manny. "I think Mrs. York's customers will like it, too."

C. Think about it.

Why do people care about the color of the building where they live, work, and have fun? Why is it helpful for a painter to understand these feelings?

A. Draw lines to match the words that rhyme.

1. other   **a.** mind

2. how   **b.** brother

3. days   **c.** now

4. find   **d.** pays

B. Read the words in the list. Read the phrases. Write the correct word after the phrase that tells about it.

company
her
around
after
responsible
family
new
because

1. mother, father, and children   _family_

2. a business _____

3. not before _____

4. on all sides _____

5. tells why _____

6. not him _____

7. just made _____

8. a worker you can depend on _____

C. Write the word company for each picture.

1. You are good ___company___, Kay.

2. Stan works for the Sun Van Lines _____.

3. April and her sons are having _____.

Sight Words

A. Read the phrases in the box aloud. Practice until you can read them smoothly.

1. in her business
2. decided on white walls
3. not possible
4. pick the paint color
5. Under the rules of these buildings
6. all done
7. work faster
8. painting over any marks on the wall
9. made the worn walls

B. Write the phrases to complete the story.

What colors did April use ———— in her business ————?
1

Most people ————————————————
2

for their apartments. In some buildings it was ————————
3

———————— for people to ————————————————.
4

————————————————————————————
5

————————————, the walls were ———————— in the same
6

color. April could ———————— in ————————
7   8

————————————————————————————.

She ———————————————— look like new.
9

C. Read the story aloud. Practice until you can read it smoothly.

5

Unit 1

A. Choose a consonant or consonants from the boxes below. Put the letters in the circle to make words with <u>-ark</u> and <u>-orn</u>. Write the words.

b
l
p
sh

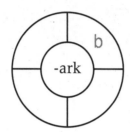

1. ____bark____

2. _____

3. _____

4. _____

c
h
t
th

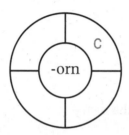

1. ____corn____

2. _____

3. _____

4. _____

B. Find another word with <u>-ark</u> or <u>-orn</u> in the words below. Circle the words and write them.

1. t(horn)   ____horn____

2. spark   _____

3. scorn   _____

4. shark   _____

5. sworn   _____

6. Clark   _____

C. Read each sentence. Circle the words that have the <u>-ark</u> or <u>-orn</u> sound. Write them.

1. (Mark) asked April to paint his home the color of (corn) because it made him think of summer. ____Mark____ ____corn____

2. Mrs. Stark wanted her walls to be a light cream color.

   _____

3. "Paint my den a dark tan," said Mr. Horn. _____

   _____

4. With a spark in her eye, April said, "I could have sworn you would want red." _____ _____

A. Read the words in the list. All the words have the vowel sound heard in <u>her</u>. Write the words from the list in which the underlined vowel sound is spelled:

person
girl
purse
nurse
permission
first

1. er   _____person_____   _____

2. ir   _____   _____

3. ur   _____   _____

B. Read each word pair aloud. Circle the word that has the vowel sound heard in <u>art</u>. Write it.

1. stand   (start)   _____start_____

2. hard   hat   _____

3. farm   fan   _____

C. Read each word pair aloud. Circle the word that has the vowel sound heard in <u>for</u>. Write it.

1. cook   cork   _____

2. horn   house   _____

3. boy   born   _____

D. Read each sentence. Circle the words that have a vowel followed by <u>r</u>. Write the words.

1. One of the (first) things people told April was the (color) they had in mind. _____first_____ _____color_____

2. April liked this part of her job. _____

_____

3. She was a responsible person and didn't mind long, hard days.

_____ _____

4. April liked to start the day at 7 A.M. _____

A. Write the plural form for each noun by adding -es.

1. address   _addresses_   2. bus   _____

3. grass   _____   4. boss   _____

5. sickness   _____   6. box   _____

B. Write the correct form of the verb for each phrase. Then write your own sentence using the phrase.

1. she (wish, wishes)   _wishes_

_____

_____

2. they (fix, fixes)   _____

_____

_____

3. he (relax, relaxes)   _____

_____

_____

4. you (teach, teaches)   _____

_____

_____

C. Write the correct form of the word for each sentence.

1. April checks the   _addresses_   of her jobs before she leaves home.
   address

2. When Mr. Baker has the van, April has to take the   _____
   to her jobs.   **bus**

3. Mr. Baker is one of the best   _____ April has had.
   boss

4. He   _____ her a lot about paint colors.
   teach

8

Fact and Opinion

A. Read the rest of the story.

The Colors of a Sunset

Mrs. Lee wanted dark green paint on her walls. "Green makes me think of the grass in the park," she said. "I can't get around too well now, and I miss the park."

April looked at the worn walls of the small apartment. She wanted to do what Mrs. Lee wanted, but she didn't think dark green was the best color to pick. "Did you know that dark colors make apartments look smaller?" she asked.

Mrs. Lee thought about that. "This apartment is small," she said. "Maybe you're right. Well, would it be possible to use olive green?"

April thought fast. Olive was not much better. It might not be a very cheerful color. April didn't like to think of the older woman alone in a drab apartment. "Have you seen the park in the spring?" she asked. "Do you remember the colors?"

"Why, yes," said Mrs. Lee. "The colors are new and light then. They are full of hope."

"Right!" said April. "Wouldn't those colors look nice in your apartment? They would make you think of spring and all the lovely days that come with it. We could use light pink, lime green, and pale blue."

Mrs. Lee clapped her hands. "April, what a good idea. I would love those colors. It's decided then. I hope you can start right away."

April nodded. "I'll talk to my boss, Mr. Baker. Then we'll get under way."

As she walked back to the van, April smiled. For last week's customer she had painted the colors of a sunset, and for this week's customer she'd be using the colors of spring. What would it be the week after? She couldn't wait to find out.

B. Read the sentences below. Write F for <u>fact</u> and O for <u>opinion</u>.

_____ **1.** Dark colors can make a home look smaller.

_____ **2.** Spring is the best time of year.

_____ **3.** Tan walls are better than gray walls.

_____ **4.** Mr. Baker is April's boss.

A. Write your own story about the colors you would want April to use if she painted your house, apartment, or business. Which colors would you use in the different rooms and why? You may want to use the words and phrases below in the box.

Words	Phrases
experienced	color of the sky
references	silver and gold
apartments	like green grass
	the colors look like
	what is around me
	warm and cool colors

_____

_____

_____

_____

_____

_____

_____

_____

_____

_____

_____

_____

_____

B. Read your story. Did you make your opinions clear? Did you add facts? Check to see if your story is clear to a reader. Go back and make the changes you need.

READING AND DISCUSSING

A. Talk about it.

Do you have a car? How do you get around? Do you like to drive? Why or why not?

B. Read the story.

Buying a Car

Stan wanted a car. He had been working for a year and had saved some money. Now he thought he could buy one.

"I can use it for dates, and I can drive it to work," he told his older brother Ray. "I can take you and Star around, too. Maybe I can take Star to the clinic when the baby comes."

"That would be helpful, Stan," said Ray. "We can't buy a car of our own now. We're still paying for our new bedroom set."

"I'm going to get the best car there is," bragged Stan. "I don't want to think about cost. I'm tired of thinking about how much things cost. I'm tired of being a small fry."

"Good luck!" laughed Ray. "I hope you have a lot of money in the bank. You're going to need it. They don't give things away, you know. And if you don't pay all at once, you will have to pay interest. That way the car will cost you more in the long run. You have to know what you're doing when you shop, Stan."

"No problem," said Stan. "Money talks."

"It does help to have the money," said Ray, "but you still have to watch how much you spend. Think about what you're getting for your money. It pays to shop around for the best value."

"I'm not much of a shopper," said Stan. "I bet I can find just what I'm looking for at the right price."

"Good luck!" said Ray.

C. Think about it.

What things must you think about if you want to get the best buy for your money? What does Stan mean when he says, "I'm tired of being a small fry"?

Review Words

A. Draw lines to match the words that rhyme.

1. wife   **a.** string

2. spend   **b.** late

3. bring   **c.** blend

4. save   **d.** life

5. straight   **e.** gave

B. Read the clues. Choose words from the list to complete the puzzle.

baby
guitar
pregnant
cost
customer
coupon
company

Across

1. a business
4. someone who buys
   in a store
5. a small child
7. price; what you pay

Down

2. about to have a child
3. you play music on it
   with your hands
6. helps you save money
   on food

C. Write sentences using the review words.

1. _____

_____

2. _____

_____

3. _____

_____

Sight Words

A. Read the phrases in the box aloud. Practice until you can read them smoothly.

1. to buy furniture
2. can afford a pretty little car
3. for months
4. So Stan checks out
5. It is plain
6. about credit and interest
7. Yes, he likes the cars
8. names the cost

B. Write the phrases to complete the story.

Stan doesn't want _____
                                        1

like his brother and sister-in-law did. He isn't a family man, and

he wants to spend his money on fun things. Stan thinks he

_____
                      2

because he has saved _____. _____
                              3   4

_____ some of the newest cars.

_____ that Stan doesn't know much
          5

_____. _____
     6   7

_____, but when Mr. Knight

_____, Stan is in shock.
          8

C. Read the story aloud. Practice until you can read it smoothly.

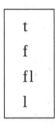

same

came

blame

gain

main

strain

A. Read the words in the list. They all have the long <u>a</u> sound. Write <u>-ain</u> or <u>-ame</u> to make words with the long <u>a</u> sound.

1. n _____*ame*_____   2. p _____

3. br _____   4. fr _____

B. Choose a consonant or consonants from the boxes below. Put the letters in the circle to make words with the long <u>a</u> sound. Write the words.

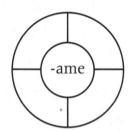

1. _____

2. _____

3. _____

4. _____

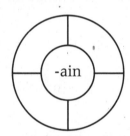

1. _____

2. _____

3. _____

4. _____

C. Read each word pair aloud. Circle the word with the long <u>a</u> sound. Write it.

1. good   game   _____

2. store   stain   _____

3. plain   plan   _____

D. Read each sentence. Circle the words with the long <u>a</u> sound. Write them.

1. When Stan came to the car lot, he walked over to a long black

car. _____

2. It was plain to see that he liked the black one. _____

3. It was a shame that the car cost so much. _____

maid
pain
take
rage
way
stay

A. Read the words in the list. They all have the long <u>a</u> sound. Write <u>-aid</u>, <u>-ape</u>, or <u>-age</u> to make words with the long <u>a</u> sound.

1. gr _____   **2.** p _____

3. p _____   **4.** w _____

B. Choose a consonant or consonants from the boxes below. Put the letters in the circle to make words with the long <u>a</u> sound. Write the words.

m
br
p
r

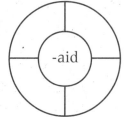

1. _____

2. _____

3. _____

4. _____

t
c
g
dr

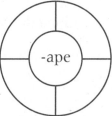

1. _____

2. _____

3. _____

4. _____

p
st
s
c

-age

1. _____

2. _____

3. _____

4. _____

C. Read each word pair aloud. Circle the word that has the long <u>a</u> sound. Write it.

1. braid   brag   _____

2. group   gray   _____

3. plate   plight   _____

4. drape   drug   _____

5. rain   ran   _____

Comparisons

A. Fill in the chart. Write the missing form of each word.

	-er	**-est**
1. old	older	oldest
2. plain	plainer	
3. new		newest
4. light	lighter	
5.	grayer	grayest
6. bold		boldest
7. thick	thicker	
8. clean		cleanest

B. Read the paragraph. Circle the words that compare things.

Stan looked at lots of cars. Some were smaller than others. Some were slicker, too. The slickest car of all was the black one. The seats were blue with deeper blue mats. Stan thought it was the neatest car in the lot.

C. Write the correct word in each sentence.

1. Stan looked at used cars. Some were _____
   old   older   oldest
   than others.

2. A few cars were not too clean. The_____ car
   clean   cleaner   cleanest
   in the lot was the blue one.

3. "I want the _____ car you have," Stan told
   new   newer   newest
   the man there.

4. "That would be the blue jeep. But the red car is

   _____ than the jeep," said Mr. Knight.
   quick   quicker   quickest

Comparing and Contrasting

A. Read the rest of the story.

Buying a Car

Stan went home to think about the cars he had checked out. If he got a new one, it was plain that he would have to buy on credit. Then he would pay interest. He would have the car he wanted most, but his monthly payments would be pretty big. It would take a big part of his paycheck. There wouldn't be much to spend on things like furniture, movies, and eating out. He couldn't afford many dates with his friend Jill.

How Stan wanted that black car! But something told him not to make up his mind too quickly. "Why buy a car if I can't afford to keep it or use it?" he asked.

So Stan shopped around some more. He looked at vans and jeeps as well as cars. They all cost more money than Stan had saved.

Stan went back to the used car lot. The man let him drive a few cars around. The blue one wasn't bad. "This car is in good shape," the man said. Stan could see that he was right. This was a car he could afford, too. He could buy the car from his savings right now and pay for the upkeep and insurance with his wages.

"Someday," said Stan, "I'll buy a new car, the one I want most. But I can see that this isn't the time for me to do that yet. For now the blue car will have to do."

B. Write the answers to the questions. Use complete sentences.

1. How are the black and blue cars different?

_____

_____

2. In what way are the black and blue cars alike?

_____

_____

3. How is buying the blue car different from buying the black one?

_____

_____

A. Write your own story about buying something important. What was it? How long did it take you to get it? Did you get a good buy? You may want to use the words and phrases in the box below.

Words	Phrases
payment	pretty good credit
total	monthly payments
insurance	fine new furniture
	can afford so little
	checking out name brands

_____

_____

_____

_____

_____

_____

_____

_____

_____

_____

_____

_____

_____

B. Read your story. Did it come out the way you wanted it to? Check your spelling. Did you add <u>-er</u> and <u>-est</u> when you compared things? Go back and make the changes you need.

READING AND DISCUSSING

A. Talk about it.

Who are your favorite musicians? What kinds of music do they play?

B. Read the story.

Selena and Her Music

When Selena died in 1995, it sent a shock wave through the world of music. It was sad to lose a young woman who had been making an old kind of music popular. The music is called Tejano.

As a musical style, Tejano began about a hundred years ago in south Texas. At that time, many newcomers from foreign countries came to work on Texas farms and ranches side by side with workers from Mexico. To have some fun after a long, hard day, people from these different places began to put their music and their instruments together. The workers from Mexico used mainly the drum, the guitar, and the flute. The other workers brought in the accordian. The rhythms, styles, and musical traditions blended quickly, and Tejano music was born.

Tejano has been a long-time favorite in Texas. Through the years, many fine musicians have played Tejano and added other sounds and instruments to it, like disco and keyboard. What Selena was doing was making Tejano fans out of music-lovers in other places. Selena was able to do this because she believed in herself as well as in the music.

C. Think about it.

What makes a star a star? Is it <u>who</u> they are, <u>what</u> they do, or something of both? What is your definition of the word <u>star</u>?

A. Read the words in the list and listen for the number of syllables in each word. Write the word in the correct column.

players
fans
countries
meet
people
together

One Syllable	Two Syllables	Three Syllables
_____	_____	_____
_____	_____	_____
_____	_____	_____

B. Write the words in alphabetical order.

1. tune   1. _different_
2. different   2. _____
3. records   3. _____
4. group   4. _____
5. listen   5. _____
6. meet   6. _____
7. people   7. _____
8. enjoy   8. _____

C. Write the word <u>meet</u> for each picture.

1. Will our team win the track _____?

2. "It's nice to _____ you!"

3. Can he make ends _____?

Sight Words

A. Read the phrases in the box aloud. Practice until you can read them smoothly.

1. around the world
2. musicians combine styles
3. rhythms and melodies
4. different traditions
5. musical instruments
6. are popular
7. old tunes
8. may have died out
9. may become part of

B. Write the phrases to complete the story.

All _____ 1 , _____ 2

_____ they learn from one another.

In this way the _____ 3 of

_____ 4 come together

in a new way. The _____ 5 that

_____ 6 in one country are soon popular in

others as well. The _____ 7 that _____ 8

_____ in one place _____ 9

a new kind of music.

C. Read the story aloud. Practice until you can read it smoothly.

Phonics   -ie and -ice

lie
nice
vie
cried
price
splice

A. Read the words in the list. They all have the long <u>i</u> sound. Write <u>-ie</u> or <u>-ice</u> to make words with the long <u>i</u> sound.

1. t _____

2. m _____

3. tw _____

4. p _____

B. Choose a consonant or consonants from the boxes below. Put the letters in the circle to make words with the long <u>i</u> sound. Write the words.

t
d
l
p

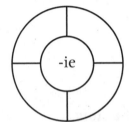

1. _____

2. _____

3. _____

4. _____

r
sp
v
sl

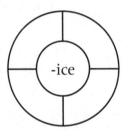

1. _____

2. _____

3. _____

4. _____

C. Read each word pair aloud. Circle the word with the long <u>i</u> sound. Write it.

1. die   did   _____

2. slay   slice   _____

3. maid   mice   _____

4. price   pretty   _____

D. Read each sentence. Circle the <u>-ice</u> and <u>-ie</u> words. Write them.

1. That record is worth the price. _____

2. The guitar makes a nice sound. _____

3. They tried to splice the tape to get the best parts.

_____ _____

lie
like
shine
shy
fry
find
right
sunlight

A. Read the words in the list. They all have the long i sound. Write -ind, -ive, or ight to make words with the long i sound.

1. dr _____

2. m _____

3. m _____

4. br _____

B. Choose a consonant or consonants from the boxes below. Put the letters in the circle to make words with the long i sound. Write the words.

b
gr
k

-ind

1. _____

2. _____

3. _____

m
sl
t

-ight

1. _____

2. _____

3. _____

C. Add the letters at the left to the endings to form words with the long i sound.

sl +
-y
-ice
-ight

1. _____sly_____

2. _____

3. _____

f +
-ine
-ive
-ight

1. _____

2. _____

3. _____

D. Read each sentence. Circle the long i word. Write it.

1. A lot of people thrive on good music. _____

2. They pick the sound that's right for them. _____

A. Read the letter. Find the parts of the letter that are missing. Write the parts from the box in the correct places in the letter.

Dear Joy	**Lana**
Oct.1, 2000	**Your friend**

(month, day, year) _____

(Opening) _____,

    You'll never guess what I found on my day off! I went to a yard sale on the next street, and there in a big pile were a lot of CDs for $1.00 each. I bought two really great ones by Selena. These are the first things I'll play for you when you visit me because I know you're a Selena fan!

(Closing) _____,

_____

B. Write the answers to the questions. Use complete sentences.

1. Where did Lana go on her day off?

   _____

   _____

2. What did Lana find that made her happy?

   _____

   _____

3. How much did Lana pay?

   _____

   _____

4. Why will Lana play the CDs for Joy?

   _____

   _____

A. Read the rest of the story.

Selena and Her Music

Selena began singing and performing at the age of ten. Her father had been a member of a band. As Selena grew up, that band became hers. Many members of her family were part of the band. Her brother played and wrote songs for her. Her sister was the drummer. Selena's husband played lead guitar. But Selena seemed to be the power-house behind it all. Her fans say she was so full of pep and happiness that everyone got caught up in her spell. One fan said that she would just step on stage and take over.

Selena's work didn't stop with music. One thing she worked at was talking to teenage girls about staying in school and getting the skills they needed to make a good living. To do this, she went back often to the high school she had gone to. There, Selena told the girls, "Hey, stay in school! Get the best education you can!"

One student said she had never felt good about herself until Selena talked to her. The student wanted a career in art. Selena said to her, "You can do it! If that's what you like, you can do it. Just try a little harder!" That student finished high school and went on to learn more about art.

Tejano music got a big lift from Selena. Many people got a big lift from her, too.

B. Write 1, 2, and 3 to show the correct order of events.

_____ Tejano music is born.

_____ At the age of ten, Selena works with a band.

_____ Selena helps girls stay in school.

C. Underline the words that best complete the sentence.

Tejano music became very popular outside of Texas

1. before Selena was born.

2. after Selena died.

3. while Selena was singing it.

A. Write your own story about a music star. Who is the star? What kind of music does she or he play? Why do you like this star and his or her music? You may want to use the words and phrases in the box below.

Words	Phrases
musicians	the melodies I like
songs	a way to combine styles
popular	a tradition where I come from
style	things that have died out
instruments	all around the world
rhythms	where I live

_____

_____

_____

_____

_____

_____

_____

_____

_____

_____

_____

_____

_____

_____

B. Read your story. Did you add details? Check to see if you told things in the order that they happened. Go back and make the changes you need.

READING AND DISCUSSING

A. Talk about it.

How safe is the block where you live?

B. Read the story.

What Can We Do?

Mr. Price:	Well, kids, how was school today?
Fran:	All the kids and teachers had a big meeting. Some people talked to us about how to stay safe when we're on our own.
Brad:	They gave us all kinds of tips, but we know all that. We can keep out of trouble.
Mr. Price:	Sometimes trouble has a way of finding you, Brad. I think we've got problems right on our own block.
Fran:	Why? What's been going on?
Mr. Price:	Hope Chin was mugged at the north end of the block this month. Mrs. Sweet had to put cameras in her store to keep an eye on everything. Little Jean Clay had some trouble at the library, too. It's a shame. This used to be a nice street.
Brad:	Well, I think it still is.
Fran:	Why don't we talk to the people who live and work here? We could have a meeting like the one at school.
Mr. Price:	Maybe we should. We can't afford to let the block get run down.
Fran:	Right! We won't wait for more trouble. We'll do something before it's too late.

C. Think about it.

How can people work together to overcome their problems?

Review Words

every
or
club
late
around
once
always

A. Use the number code to write the words.

a	b	c	d	e	f	g	h	i	j	k	l	m
1	2	3	4	5	6	7	8	9	10	11	12	13

n	o	p	q	r	s	t	u	v	w	x	y	z
14	15	16	17	18	19	20	21	22	23	24	25	26

11 9 4 19 _____   14 5 22 5 18 _____

13 5 1 14 _____   3 15 21 12 4 _____

B. Look down and across in the box. Find the words from the list and then circle them. Write them.

o	a	l	w	a	y	s
p	z	s	c	o	z	c
g	o	q	l	a	t	e
a	r	o	u	n	d	l
k	s	n	b	h	z	b
x	t	c	b	q	m	q
e	v	e	r	y	f	i

1. _____ always
2. _____
3. _____
4. _____
5. _____
6. _____
7. _____

C. Write the word party for each picture.

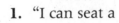

1. "I can seat a _____ of two."

2. "This is a good _____!"

3. "Our _____ will win."

Sight Words

A. Read the phrases in the box aloud. Practice until you can read them smoothly.

1. isn't very safe
2. they worry when they see strangers around
3. don't want to go out alone
4. kind of like a small town
5. to protect our families and friends
6. guard what we own
7. must show any troublemakers
8. they'll have to watch out
9. our grounds

B. Write the phrases to complete the story.

If people think a street _____ then

1

_____ .

2

People who live on the block _____

3

_____ .

"A city street is _____ ,"

4

Mr. Price said. "We want _____

5

_____ and _____ .

6

We _____

7

that we mean it. When they're on our block,

_____ ! These are

8

_____ , and we'll work to keep our

9

street a good place to live and work."

C. Read the story aloud. Practice until you can read it smoothly.

Phonics   -ound and -own

A. Choose a consonant or consonants from the box below. Put the letters in the circle to make words with -ound. Write the words.

gr
h
f
r
s

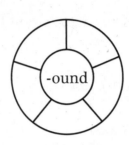

1. _____
2. _____
3. _____
4. _____
5. _____

B. Add the letters from the box below to -own to form new words. Write them.

cl
fr
br
cr
dr

+   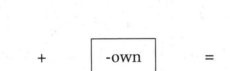   =

1. _____
2. _____
3. _____
4. _____
5. _____

C. Read each sentence. Circle the words with -ound or -own. Write them.

1. Mr. Price pounded the table. _____

2. After that there wasn't a sound in the room. _____

3. "We can't let this block run down," he told the group.

   _____

4. "Working together is bound to help." _____

5. "We can get a guard at night to watch the stores in town,"

   said Brad. _____

6. "We'll make this street the safest one around," said Fran.

   _____

shout	found	own	coupon
how	grow	soup	vow
group	town	sprout	show
pound	blow	cow	you

A. Read the words in the box above. Write the words from the box that have the vowel sound described below.

1. the vowel sound in <u>out</u> spelled <u>ou</u>

   shout _____ _____ _____

2. the vowel sound in <u>out</u> spelled <u>ow</u>

   how _____ _____ _____

3. the vowel sound in <u>no</u> spelled <u>ow</u>

   own _____ _____ _____

4. the vowel sound in <u>to</u> spelled <u>ou</u>

   coupon _____ _____ _____

B. Read each sentence. Circle all the words with <u>-ou</u> and <u>-ow</u>. Write them.

1. The people in the block south of ours got together to work as

   a group. _____ _____ _____

2. They have found that their block is safer now.

   _____ _____

3. We must ask them how they worked out their plan.

   _____ _____

4. We need to know how to keep our own block safe, too.

   _____ _____ _____ _____

5. When you can show others that it pays to work together,

   they'll join your group. _____ _____

   _____ _____

Adding Endings to -y Words

A. Fill in the chart. Write the missing form of each word.

	-ies	**-ied**
1. try	tries	
2. carry		carried
3.	cries	cried
4. fry	fries	
5. spy		spied
6. worry	worries	
7.	dries	dried

B. Read the paragraph. Circle the words that end in -ies and -ied.

Brad spied someone he didn't know waiting around the library. He tried to watch as the man went down the street. "He carries a brown bag," thought Brad. "Should I try to find out what is in it? Every time I get near him, he shies away." Brad worried about the stranger all day.

C. Complete each sentence with the correct word.

1. Hope Chin _____ when someone took her money.
   cry   cried

2. Now she _____ her money out of sight.
   carry   carries

3. The new group works for our block and _____
   try   tries
   to keep it safe.

4. Everyone was so _____ before the group got
   worries   worried
   together, but things are much better now.

Inference

A. Read the rest of the story.

What Can We Do?

"Brad, I have a job for you and Fran," Mr. Price said. "We're all interested in keeping our block safe. Why don't you talk to Mrs. Browning and the group she got together to help stop crime? They should have some good ideas about making our street safer."

"We're ahead of you this time, Dad," said Brad. "We've talked to Mrs. Browning, and she jotted down this list of tips." Brad handed the page to his father, and Mr. Price quickly scanned the list.

1. Talk to cops about ways to stop crime.

2. Ask parents to teach children who are alone not to talk to any strangers on the street.

3. Ask everyone to watch out for the kids on the block.

4. Find ways to make money to pay for a guard when one is needed.

5. Ask store owners to call for help if people are in trouble out on the street.

"This kind of list can help all of us," said Mr. Price. "Fran, you and Brad show everyone these tips. If all of us do the things on the list, we won't have to worry about being safe. Something tells me that working together will pay off very well and will be fun, too."

B. List some important facts about the story.

1. _____

2. _____

3. _____

C. Underline the best inference about the story.

1. Nothing can be done to help people stay safe.

2. When it comes to safety, people can't let down their guard.

3. Mrs. Browning's group was not helpful.

From Reading to Writing

A. Write your own story about a problem that you needed the help of other people to solve. What was the problem? How did you work it out? What was your job? You may want to use the words and phrases in the box below.

Words	Phrases
telephone	any kind of problem
number	watch out for strangers in this town
emergency	very worried
address	can't do it alone
	show how to clean up the grounds

_____

_____

_____

_____

_____

_____

_____

_____

_____

_____

_____

_____

B. Read your story aloud. Is your main idea clear? How can you improve it? Check to see if you spelled words correctly when you added endings to -y words. Make any changes you need.

READING AND DISCUSSING

A. Talk about it.

What kinds of hopes and plans do people have when they come to a new country?

B. Read the story.

From City Streets

In 1974 Om Dutta Sharma and his wife left their home in India to come to the United States. Like many newcomers, they hoped for a better life. And like many others, they found it was hard going at first. Mrs. Sharma was a nurse and soon found work. Mr. Sharma had learned law, but he did not know American law. So he worked at different jobs. However, none of them lasted long. Then one day he got a job as a cab driver.

Mr. Sharma loved being a cab driver. His working day was long, and he worked seven days a week. But as he drove around the city, he talked and laughed with the customers in his cab. He loved being free to say whatever he thought. Mr. Sharma also liked helping people. Sometimes he gave free rides to old people. Sometimes he sent money back to India to help people there.

The years went by. The Sharmas had two children. The family had the things it needed like food and a home, but Mr. Sharma did not spend a lot of money on other things. He did not take his wife out to eat or buy her pretty dresses. Mr. Sharma was very careful with his money because he had a plan.

C. Think about it.

Why do people work hard? Is it just for money?

Review Words

A. Read the words in the first list. Look for smaller words within each word. Write the word from the list that contains:

attention
about
customer

1. the word <u>us</u>   _____

2. the word <u>tent</u>   _____

3. the word <u>out</u>   _____

4. the word <u>at</u>   _____

B. Read the clues. Choose words from the second list to complete the puzzle.

when
time
found
night
watched

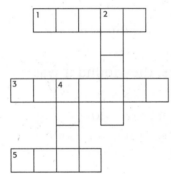

Across

1. opposite of lost
3. looked at
5. rhymes with then

Down

2. opposite of day
4. what a clock tells

C. Use the number code to write the words.

a	b	c	d	e	f	g	h	i	j	k	l	m
1	2	3	4	5	6	7	8	9	10	11	12	13

n	o	p	q	r	s	t	u	v	w	x	y	z
14	15	16	17	18	19	20	21	22	23	24	25	26

19 8 15 23   16 21 20

_____   _____

15 14 5   13 15 14 20 8

_____   _____

14 9 7 8 20   23 8 5 14

_____   _____

Sight Words

A. Read the phrases in the box aloud. Practice until you can read them smoothly.

> 1. really finds joy
> 2. answer to a boss or take orders
> 3. very famous people
> 4. success comes
> 5. just talking on impulse
> 6. feel like failures
> 7. help those customers out
> 8. spoil his day
> 9. the programs

B. Write the phrases to complete the story.

Mr. Sharma _____ in his work.

1

He doesn't have to _____

2

_____ from one. Sometimes Mr. Sharma picks up

_____. His _____

3   **4**

from _____ to people in his cab.

5

If people are down or _____, Mr.

6

Sharma tries to _____ with a good

7

talk. When a rude customer tries to _____, Mr.

8

Sharma thinks about _____ he can pay for in India.

9

C. Read the story aloud. Practice until you can read it smoothly.

A. Choose a consonant or consonants from the boxes below. Put the letters in the circle to make words with -oil and -oy. Write the words.

b
c
f
s

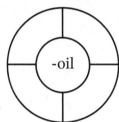

1. _____

2. _____

3. _____

4. _____

j
t
c
Tr

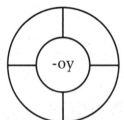

1. _____

2. _____

3. _____

4. _____

B. Read each group of words. Circle the word with the -oil or -oy sound. Write it.

1. spot   spoil   spill   _____

2. foil   fill   fell   _____

3. ploy   plan   plot   _____

4. braid   brow   broil   _____

5. club   cloy   clown   _____

C. Complete each sentence with a word that has the -oil or -oy sound.

1. The Sharmas have two _____ of their own.
   boys   boxes

2. They didn't _____ their children by buying them
   spoil   spot
   everything they wanted.

3. The Sharma children did not have every _____ they
   toy   top
   saw on TV.

4. Mr. Sharma's father farmed in India, but the _____
   soil   soy
   was not good.

Phonics   -oi and -oy

A. Read the words in the list. They all have the -oi and -oy sound.
Write -oi or -oy to make words with these sounds.

oil
join
noise
point
boy
loyal

1. c _____ l   2. enj _____

3. t _____   4. sp _____ l

B. Read each group of words. Circle the word with the -oi or -oy sound.
Write it.

1. told   toil   time   _____

2. cry   cot   coy   _____

3. soil   sell   soon   _____

4. poison   prison   pop   _____

5. old   oily   once   _____

C. Complete each sentence with the word that has the -oi or -oy sound.

1. Mr. Sharma doesn't think of his work as _____.
                                            tote   toil

2. He doesn't mind all the _____ of the city.
                            noise   nose

3. People in a hurry don't get him _____.
                                    upset   annoyed

4. He keeps spare _____ in a box under the car seat.
                   coins   cones

D. Read each sentence. Circle the word with -oi or -oy. Write it.

1. A cab driver has to make choices about what streets to take.

   _____

2. Many newcomers are still loyal to their home country.

   _____

3. Mr. Sharma is employed driving his own his cab. _____

4. Mr. Sharma points out things of interest to his customers.

   _____

A. Write the plural possessive form of each noun.

1. drivers   the _____drivers'_____ meeting

2. kids   the _____ toys

3. brothers   the _____ parents

4. workers   the _____ paychecks

B. Some of the nouns below are singular and some are plural. Write the correct possessive.

1. shoppers   two _____ bags

2. grandmother   my _____ dishes

3. customers   those _____ rides

4. wife   my _____ ticket

5. learners   those _____ needs

C. Read the paragraphs. Circle the plural words that show ownership.

Down the long street, the lights' color turns from red to green.
Cars, vans, and buses zip by. Trucks' loud horns add to the noise.
Everyone wants to go somewhere fast.

Mr. Sharma keeps his customers' needs in mind as he drives
around the city. He stops for two women. The shoppers' boxes and
bags fill the cab. The women's voices fill his ears as they tell him
about their buys. Soon the cab pulls up to a big building, and the
women get out. The riders' fares and tips go in Mr. Sharma's wallet.

D. Write your own phrases. Use the words as plural possessives.

1. peoples   _____

2. girls   _____

3. teachers   _____

A. Read the rest of the story.

From City Streets

Mr. Sharma had come from a town in India that was not very big. Most people were farmers and not at all well-off. There was no phone in the whole town. Mr. Sharma's mother still lived there, so from time to time, he went back to see her. Then in 1996, Mr. Sharma's mother died. What would become of the house where she had lived?

The answer was a really good plan. Mr. Sharma gave money to set up a school in his old home. The school was for girls in first to fifth grade. The school was named for Mr. Sharma's mother who had never learned to read and write. In India, many girls in farming towns do not get the chance to go to school. Those girls do not know the joy of learning to read.

Mr. Sharma sends money each year to pay for the school. The girls sit on the floor to do their work. If it is a fine day, the girls sometimes sit on the roof of the building. The school has five teachers. Soon, the school will add more programs in order to take girls up to the tenth grade.

Why does Mr. Sharma give so much of his money to this town in India? He feels he has been lucky to have success in his own life. "You are always getting, getting, getting," he says. "You have to give it back."

B. Use facts from the story to answer the questions.

1. Why do you think Mr. Sharma set up a school for girls?

_____

_____

2. How does Mr. Sharma feel about money? How does he feel about life?

_____

_____

From Reading to Writing

A. How do you feel about Mr. Sharma's experience? What would you like to do for others? Write your own story about working hard, getting, and giving something back. You may want to use the words and phrases in the box below.

Words	Phrases
meaning	giving to others
failure	helping people
choices	not get spoiled
answers	good impulses
famous	different kinds of success

_____

_____

_____

_____

_____

_____

_____

_____

_____

_____

_____

_____

B. Read your story. Check to see if you wrote all your possessive nouns correctly. Go back and make the changes you need.

Deciding About a New Country

READING AND DISCUSSING

A. Talk about it.

Do you have family who live a long distance away? Does being separated from them make you feel lonely?

B. Read the story.

Away From the Family

I write to my family a lot, sometimes once a day. They like to hear from me and know that I'm well. I tell them what I think they want to hear.

It was hard for them to let me go, but they did because they thought my coming here was the best thing for me. In my country there aren't many chances for a woman to get ahead. I didn't want to stay and work on the farm. I wanted to get away and learn more, do new things, be someone!

To my family back home, I've done all those things. No one in my family makes as much money as I do. No one lives the way I do. No one has a home like mine. Yet what they don't know is that life is sometimes hard for me here. It is so very different from my country.

Now my brother says he wants to join me here. But there are many things for him to think about before coming here. He'll have to get a green card and learn the skills for a job in the city. He'll have to learn to get by without most of his family and the country he knows. Will he be lonely? Will my parents be upset if he comes here?

I don't know what to tell my brother. Come and take your chances, or stay with our parents and enjoy the life you have? Oh, it would be so good to have him here.

C. Think about it.

Should the woman tell her brother to come or to stay at home? Why is it sometimes hard to know what to do?

Review Words

A. Draw a line to match the word with its opposite.

1. then   **a.** there

2. here   **b.** after

3. before   **c.** now

B. Read the words in the first list. Write the words from the list in alphabetical order.

if
blues
been
sweeping
picked

1. _____

2. _____

3. _____

4. _____

5. _____

C. Read the clues. Choose words from the second list to complete the puzzle.

sentence
think
year
cooking

Down

1. 12 months
3. heating food to eat

Across

2. a group of words
4. give thought to

D. Write sentences using the review words.

1. _____

_____

2. _____

_____

Sight Words

A. Read the phrases in the box aloud. Practice until you can read them smoothly.

1. will call my family
2. to come visit me
3. at my house as long as he needs to
4. If all goes well
5. to draw up the legal papers
6. American immigration
7. my employer will give me permission
8. very new to all this

B. Write the phrases to complete the story.

I _____ this Sunday night and
                1

ask my brother _____ in this
                   2

country. He can stay _____
                     3

_____. _____
                     4

_____, he can find someone _____
                     5

_____ needed for _____
                     6

_____. I hope _____
                     7

_____ to take some

time off. My brother is _____
                   8

and will need lots of help.

C. Read the story aloud. Practice until you can read it smoothly.

A. Choose a consonant from the box below. Put the letters in the circle to make words with <u>-all</u>. Write the words.

f
c
h
t

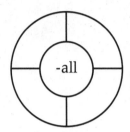

-all

1. _____

2. _____

3. _____

4. _____

B. Add the letters from the box to <u>-aw</u> to form words. Write the words.

dr
cl
fl
r
str

   +   -aw   =

1. _____

2. _____

3. _____

4. _____

5. _____

C. Complete each sentence with a word that has <u>-all</u> or <u>-aw</u>.

1. I told my brother to quit _____ about coming to
                                      stalling   staining

   this country.

2. At first it was like talking to a brick _____.
                                               well   wall

3. There is a lot to know about the immigration _____.
                                                       laws   lags

4. Getting a green card is no _____ deed.
                                       smell   small

5. In the long run, my brother _____ that I was right.
                                           saw   say

6. I would like to be with _____ my family, but I'm glad
                                       all   oil

   at least my brother can come here.

A. Say each word and listen for the number of syllables.

1 syllable	2 syllables	3 syllables	4 syllables
call	pa-pers	em-ploy-er	A-mer-i-can
green	le-gal	per-mis-sion	e-mer-gen-cy
house	vis-it	tel-e-phone	im-mi-gra-tion

B. Say each word. Listen for the number of syllables you hear in each one. Write the number.

1. goes _____
2. address _____
3. channel _____
4. remember _____
5. library _____
6. information _____

C. Read each word below. The syllable with the schwa sound is underlined. Circle the vowel letter that stands for the schwa sound in each syllable.

a	e	i	o	u
ⓐn-noy	par-<u>ents</u>	fam-<u>i</u>-ly	doc-<u>tor</u>	Au-<u>gust</u>
<u>a</u>-way	af-<u>ter</u>	hol-<u>i</u>-day	pris-<u>on</u>	play-<u>ful</u>

D. Look at the words again in Exercise C. Then read the sentences below. Fill in the missing syllable. Write the word.

1. My fam__i__ly likes to hear from me. _____family_____

2. They feel I have been ____way a long time. _____

3. I would like to see my par_____. _____

4. Being alone can feel like being in pris_____. _____

5. My brother will try to come here in Au_____.

   _____

6. It will be like a hol____day to see him again. _____

7. I won't _____noy my friends by moping around any more.

   _____

A. Read the list of past verbs. Write the past verb from the list next to the present verb below.

ate
wrote
ran
drew
brought
knew
fought
kept
drove
swam

1. run _____   2. draw _____

3. write _____   4. eat _____

5. swim _____   6. know _____

7. fight _____   8. keep _____

9. drive _____   10. bring _____

B. Complete each sentence with the past tense verb.

1. In a way I _____ to come to this country.
   fought   fight

2. My parents _____ me at home as long as they could.
   keep   kept

3. They _____ I wouldn't come back.
   knew   know

4. The hope of a good job _____ me away.
   draw   drew

5. This hope _____ many other people here, too.
   bring   brought

6. Like most new people, I _____ into a few problems.
   ran   run

C. Read the paragraph. Circle the verbs that show the past.

I brought some friends home from work. We ate food from my country. I drew a map of my homeland showing the big lake where I swam. The fun ran on for hours. Today I wrote to my family about the party.

D. Write a sentence using a present verb. Rewrite the sentence using a past verb.

1. _____

_____

2. _____

_____

A. Read the rest of the story.

Away From the Family

Today I got a letter from my parents. They are thinking of selling the farm. They want to come here, not for a visit, but to live in this country and become Americans.

I don't know if this is the right thing for them to do. It will be hard for people of my parents' age to get green cards. They will need employers. There will be lots of legal problems. Someone will have to draw up the legal papers. All of this will take a long time. It's hard to get the kind of permission they need for immigration.

It would be nice to have all of my family with me, but I don't think my parents would like it here. They are used to their farm and the pretty country it is in. Here they can't live on a farm. They'll have to live at my house in the city. They aren't used to the noise of a city or all that goes on in one. They don't have good skills for city jobs.

I'm going to call my family tonight. It will be the hardest call I've made. I'm going to tell them not to come right away. We all need to think about this some more. I have to give them a better idea of what their life would be like here. And they have to think more about what they would be giving up. A choice like this can be painful.

B. What conclusions can you draw from the story? Underline the words that best complete each sentence.

1. The writer is troubled because she

   a. doesn't want to clean house for company.

   b. fears her parents will think she doesn't love them when she asks them to wait.

   c. thinks the telephone call will cost too much.

2. It is likely that the writer hasn't

   a. told everything about her life in this country.

   b. sent a letter to her family for months.

   c. found a good job yet.

From Reading to Writing

A. Write your own story about a hard choice you had to make. How did you make it? What did you have to give up? What did you gain? You may want to use the words and phrases in the box below.

Words	Phrases
middle	permission to do something
form	legal papers and letters
information	employer or family
male	the American way
female	goes without saying

_____

_____

_____

_____

_____

_____

_____

_____

_____

_____

_____

_____

B. Read your story. Did you explain the problem clearly? Check to see if you used irregular verbs correctly. Go back and make any changes you need.

READING AND DISCUSSING

A. Talk about it.

Do you always have a good time in a group? Do you ever pretend you're having fun when you're not?

B. Read the story.

Joining In

April looked down at her drink. She took a few sips and tried to relax. Oh, why had she told Fran she would come here? This club was no fun. The noise was too much and the people, well, the people weren't very interesting. April ate some nuts and tried to look as if she were enjoying the music.

Her friend Fran was down at the other end of the table. She had no trouble fitting in. Fran was telling Pedro and Ana a story about her employer. Nick joined them, and soon they were all laughing and carrying on. They were having their own party. They didn't need her.

"April! What is the problem?" called Fran at one point. "Aren't you having a good time? Why don't you talk to us?"

It was just like Fran to make her look bad by calling attention to her, April thought. "Don't worry about me. I'm in fine form," she laughed.

"I'll just get up and mill around a little," she thought to herself, and as she did, she walked right into someone.

"I'm glad you did that," said the stranger, "because now you'll have to talk to me."

April looked up at a tall, friendly man. He was so cute, and he was talking to her!

C. Think about it.

Why is it sometimes hard to meet new people? Why wasn't April having a good time?

A. Draw lines to match the words that rhyme.

1. would
2. why
3. how
4. thank
5. better
6. saw
7. card

a. now
b. could
c. law
d. guard
e. my
f. sank
g. letter

B. Use the number code to write the words.

a	b	c	d	e	f	g	h	i	j	k	l	m
1	2	3	4	5	6	7	8	9	10	11	12	13

n	o	p	q	r	s	t	u	v	w	x	y	z
14	15	16	17	18	19	20	21	22	23	24	25	26

13 21 19 20 _____   1 19 11 _____

19 15 15 14 _____   20 15 15 _____

19 21 13 13 5 18 _____

C. Write the word <u>join</u> for each picture.

1. Will you

_____

me?

2. Will you

_____

hands?

3. April will

_____

our social club.

Sight Words

A. Read the phrases in the box aloud. Practice until you can read them smoothly.

1. April noticed
2. had a warm, open smile
3. her wish coming true
4. for a few minutes
5. a good start so far
6. for someone's birthday
7. would please join him
8. like a small girl
9. was getting the idea

B. Write the phrases to complete the story.

_____ that the nice-looking stranger
1

_____. She had been
2

hoping for some company. Was _____
3

so soon? They talked _____. It looked like
4

_____. When the man stood up to
5

sing _____, he asked if
6

she _____. April started
7

to feel shy, _____. But she _____
8   9

_____ that the stranger wasn't just

being nice. He really liked her!

C. Read the story aloud. Practice until you can read it smoothly.

-ue and -ew

A. Add the letters from the box below to -ue to form words. Write the words.

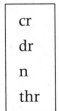

+ 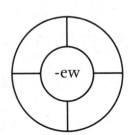 =

1. _____

2. _____

3. _____

4. _____

5. _____

B. Choose a consonant or consonants from the box below. Put the letters in the circle to make words with -ew. Write the words.

cr
dr
n
thr

-ew

1. _____

2. _____

3. _____

4. _____

C. Read each word pair aloud. Circle the word that has the same vowel sound as blue or grew. Write it.

1. truck   true   _____

2. chew   check   _____

3. brown   brew   _____

4. blew   blend   _____

5. flu   flaw   _____

D. Read each sentence. Circle the word with the same vowel sound as blue or grew. Write it.

1. As April and Troy walked outside together, Fran threw her a

   look. _____

2. Fran hadn't a clue about April and Troy. _____

3. But she could tell April wasn't blue anymore. _____

Phonics o͞o and o͝o

soup	mood	brood	blew
blue	grew	coupon	due
chew	clue	school	group

A. Read the words in the box above. All the words in the box have the same vowel sound (o͞o) as <u>food</u>. Write the words in which the vowel sound is spelled:

1. <u>ue</u> _____due_____ _____ _____

2. <u>ew</u> _____ _____ _____

3. <u>ou</u> _____ _____ _____

4. <u>oo</u> _____ _____ _____

hood	could	book	wood
would	stood	should	shook

B. Read the words in the box above. All the words in the box have the same vowel sound (o͝o) as <u>good</u>. Write the words in which the vowel sound is spelled:

1. <u>ou</u> _____could_____ _____ _____

2. <u>oo</u> _____ _____ _____

_____ _____

C. Read each word pair aloud. Circle the word that has the (o͝o) sound heard in <u>good</u>. Write it.

1. hood   hold   _____

2. brook   broil   _____

3. cope   could   _____

4. show   should   _____

6. stood   store   _____

A. Write the two words that make up each reflexive pronoun.

1. yourself _____your_____ + _____self_____

2. herself _____ + _____

3. myself _____ + _____

B. Add the plural form of self to each word. Write the new word.

1. them _____

2. our _____

3. your _____

C. Read the paragraphs. Circle the reflexive pronouns.

The day after she met Troy, April talked to Fran on the telephone. "I'm so pleased with myself," she said, "because I didn't blow it by getting shy and running away. I tend to do that."

"I'm shy sometimes myself, April," answered Fran. "Anyone can be shy, so don't be so down on yourself. Too many people make it hard for themselves when it comes to meeting someone new. That's why I joined the club. Everyone is there to meet someone. Your friend Troy was there to meet someone himself. He was glad to meet you!"

D. Use each phrase to write your own sentence.

1. by myself _____

_____

2. talking to yourself _____

_____

3. true to himself _____

_____

4. do the work ourselves _____

_____

A. Read the rest of the story.

Joining In

April started going to Fran's club. She noticed that Troy was there a lot. That made it fun because she could talk to him without making a fool of herself. She wished that she could be as warm and open as Fran. Still, little by little, she was feeling more at home in the different groups at the Downtown Club.

"How am I going to get Troy to ask me out alone?" April thought to herself. "I think he likes me, but so far I only see him here." She tried lots of things. She talked about shows that she wanted to see. She talked about parties that people were giving. She pointed out newspaper stories about where to eat. But Troy didn't ask her for a date.

"Please help me, Fran! What am I going to do? How can I get that man to ask me out?" April cried to Fran. "I mean, how can I really get to know him at the club with so many people around?"

Fran laughed, "April, that man is just as bashful as you are. Why don't you ask him out?"

April's jaw dropped. "Do you mean that?"

Fran said, "I've got an idea. His birthday is in January. It's January now, true? Ask him over for his birthday. Cook a few things for him, bake a cake!"

"Thanks, Fran!" said April. "This is a new idea for me, but I'll give it a try. After all, I'm not a shy little girl any more. You'll be the first to know how things work out."

B. Underline the best headings for facts from the story.

1. December and January

2. April's Plan and Fran's Plan

3. Birthdays and Parties

C. Put facts from the story under the headings you chose.

_____

_____

_____

From Reading to Writing

A. Write your own story about meeting someone new. Who was it? How did you meet this person? How did you feel? You may want to use the words and phrases in the box below.

Words	Phrases
menu	noticed right from the start
extras	warm and true
least	pleased to meet you
beverages	open to new ideas
	a birthday wish

_____

_____

_____

_____

_____

_____

_____

_____

_____

_____

_____

_____

B. Read your story. Did you make your point well? Check to see if you used reflexive pronouns correctly. Go back and make any changes you need.

Answer Key

Unit One

Page 4 **A.** 1. b 2. c 3. d 4. a **B.** 1. family
2. company 3. after 4. around 5. because
6. her 7. new 8. responsible **C.** 1. company
2. Company 3. company

Page 5 **B.** 1. in her business 2. decided on
white walls 3. not possible 4. pick the paint
color 5. Under the rules of these buildings
6. all done 7. work faster 8. painting over any
marks on the wall 9. made the worn walls

Page 6 **A.** 1. bark 2. lark 3. park 4. shark;
1. corn 2. horn 3. torn 4. thorn **B.** 1. horn
2. park 3. corn 4. hark 5. worn 6. lark
C. 1. Mark, corn 2. Stark 3. dark, Horn
4. spark, sworn

Page 7 **A.** 1. person, permission 2. girl, first
3. purse, nurse **B.** 1. start 2. hard 3. farm
C. 1. cork 2. horn 3. born **D.** 1. first, color
2. part, her 3. person, hard 4. start

Page 8 **A.** 1. addresses 2. bus 3. grasses
4. bosses 5. sicknesses 6. boxes **B.** 1. wishes
2. fix 3. relaxes 4. teach **C.** 1. addresses
2. buses 3. bosses 4. teaches

Page 9 **B.** 1. F 2. O 3. O 4. F

Unit Two

Page 12 **A.** 1. d 2. c 3. a 4. e 5. b
B. 1. company 2. pregnant 3. guitar
4. customer 5. baby 6. coupon 7. cost

Page 13 **B.** 1. to buy furniture 2. can
afford a pretty little car 3. for months
4. So Stan checks out 5. It is plain 6. about
credit and interest 7. Yes, he likes the cars
8. names the cost

Page 14 **A.** 1. name 2. pain 3. brain
4. frame **B.** 1. tame 2. fame 3. flame 4. lame;
1. gain 2. grain 3. train 4. vain **C.** 1. game
2. stain 3. plain **D.** 1. came 2. plain 3. shame

Page 15 **A.** 1. grape 2. paid 3. page
4. wage **B.** 1. maid 2. braid 3. paid 4. raid;
1. tape 2. cape 3. gape 4. drape; 1. page
2. stage 3. sage 4. cage **C.** 1. braid 2. gray
3. plate 4. drape 5. rain

Page 16 **A.** 1. older 2. plainest 3. newer
4. lightest 5. gray 6. bolder 7. thickest
8. cleaner **B.** smaller, slicker, slickest, deeper,
neatest **C.** 1. older 2. cleanest 3. newest
4. quicker

Page 17 **B.** 1. They are different prices
and colors. 2. They are both in good shape.
3. Stan can pay for the blue car with his
savings. He would need credit to buy the
black car.

Unit Three

Page 20 **A.** fans, meet; players, countries,
people; together **B.** different, enjoy, group,
listen, meet, people, records, tune
C. 1. meet 2. meet 3. meet

Page 21 **B.** 1. around the world
2. musicians combine styles 3. rhythms and
melodies 4. different traditions 5. musical
instruments 6. are popular 7. old tunes
8. may have died out 9. may become part of

Page 22 **A.** 1. tie 2. mice 3. twice 4. pie
B. 1. tie 2. die 3. lie 4. pie; 1. rice 2. spice
3. vice 4. slice **C.** 1. die 2. slice 3. mice
4. price **D.** 1. price 2. nice 3. tried, splice

Page 23 **A.** 1. drive 2. mind 3. might
4. bright **B.** 1. bind 2. grind 3. kind; 1. might
2. slight 3. tight **C.** 1. sly 2. slice 3. slight;
1. fine 2. five 3. fight **D.** 1. thrive 2. right

Page 24 **A.** Oct. 1, 2000; Dear Joy; Your
friend; Lana **B.** 1. She went to a yard sale.
2. She got two CDs by Selena. 3. She paid
two dollars. 4. Joy is a Selena fan.

Page 25 **B.** 1, 2, 3 **C.** 3. while Selena was
singing it

Unit Four

Page 28 **A.** kids, never, mean, could
B. Order may vary. 1. always 2. or 3. club
4. late 5. around 6. once 7. every **C.** 1. party
2. party 3. party

Page 29 **B.** 1. isn't very safe 2. they worry
when they see strangers around 3. don't
want to go out alone 4. kind of like a small
town 5. to protect our families and friends
6. guard what we own 7. must show any
troublemakers 8. they'll have to watch out
9. our grounds

Page 30 **A.** 1. ground 2. hound 3. found
4. round 5. sound **B.** 1. clown 2. frown
3. brown 4. crown 5. drown **C.** 1. pounded
2. sound 3. down 4. bound 5. town 6. around

Page 31 **A.** 1. shout, sprout, found, pound 2. how, town, cow, vow 3. own, show, grow, blow 4. coupon, group, soup, you **B.** 1. south, ours, group 2. found, now 3. how, out 4. know, how, our, own 5. you, show, your, group

Page 32 **A.** 1. tried 2. carries 3. cry 4. fried 5. spies 6. worried 7. dry **B.** spied, tried, carries, shies, worried **C.** 1. cried 2. carries 3. tries 4. worried

Page 33 **B.** 1–3. Answers will vary. **C.** 2

Unit Five

Page 36 **A.** 1. customer 2. attention 3. about 4. attention **B.** 1. found 2. night 3. watched 4. time 5. when **C.** show, put, one, month, night, when

Page 37 **B.** 1. really finds joy 2. answer to a boss or take orders 3. very famous people 4. success comes 5. just talking on impulse 6. feel like failures 7. help those customers out 8. spoil his day 9. the programs

Page 38 **A.** 1. boil 2. coil 3. foil 4. soil; 1. joy 2. toy 3. coy 4. Troy **B.** 1. spoil 2. foil 3. ploy 4. broil 5. cloy **C.** 1. boys 2. spoil 3. toy 4. soil

Page 39 **A.** 1. coil 2. enjoy 3. toy 4. spoil **B.** 1. toil 2. coy 3. soil 4. poison 5. oily **C.** 1. toil 2. noise 3. annoyed 4. coins **D.** 1. choices 2. loyal 3. employed 4. points

Page 40 **A.** 1. drivers' 2. kids' 3. brothers' 4. workers' **B.** 1. shoppers' 2. grandmother's 3. customers' 4. wife's 5. learners' **C.** lights', Trucks', customers', shoppers', women's, riders'

Page 41 **B.** 1. His mother never went to school to learn how to read and write, and he probably regretted that for her sake; he wanted to give the girls in his village a chance for an education. 2. He is willing to work hard for it, but doesn't see it as something that simply buys luxuries; he believes in using it to help others. Answers will vary. Students may say that he has a positive and unselfish attitude.

Unit Six

Page 44 **A.** 1. c 2. a 3. b **B.** 1. been 2. blues 3. if 4. picked 5. sweeping **C.** 1. year 2. sentence 3. cooking 4. think

Page 45 **B.** 1. will call my family 2. to come visit me 3. at my house as long as he needs to 4. If all goes well 5. to draw up the legal papers 6. American immigration 7. my employer will give me permission 8. very new to all this

Page 46 **A.** 1. fall 2. call 3. hall 4. tall **B.** 1. draw 2. claw 3. flaw 4. raw 5. straw **C.** 1. stalling 2. wall 3. laws 4. small 5. saw 6. all

Page 47 **B.** 1. 1 2. 2 3. 2 4. 3 5. 3 6. 4 **C.** a(n)noy, par(e)nts, fam(i)ly, doct(o)r, Aug(u)st, (a)way, aft(e)r, hol(i)day, pris(o)n, playf(u)l **D.** 1. family 2. away 3. parents 4. prison 5. August 6. holiday 7. annoy

Page 48 **A.** 1. ran 2. drew 3. wrote 4. ate 5. swam 6. knew 7. fought 8. kept 9. drove 10. brought **B.** 1. fought 2. kept 3. knew 4. drew 5. brought 6. ran **C.** brought, ate, drew, swam, ran, wrote

Page 49 **B.** 1. b 2. a

Unit Seven

Page 52 **A.** 1. b 2. e 3. a 4. f 5. g 6. c 7. d **B.** must, ask, soon, too, summer **C.** 1. join 2. join 3. join

Page 53 **B.** 1. April noticed 2. had a warm, open smile 3. her wish coming true 4. for a few minutes 5. a good start so far 6. for someone's birthday 7. would please join him 8. like a small girl 9. was getting the idea

Page 54 **A.** 1. cue 2. clue 3. glue 4. hue 5. Sue **B.** 1. crew 2. drew 3. new 4. threw **C.** 1. true 2. chew 3. brew 4. blew 5. flu **D.** 1. threw 2. clue 3. blue

Page 55 **A.** 1. due, blue, clue 2. blew, grew, chew 3. soup, coupon, group 4. mood, brood, school **B.** 1. could, would, should 2. hood, book, wood, stood, shook **C.** 1. hood 2. brook 3. could 4. should 5. stood

Page 56 **A.** 1. your, self 2. her, self 3. my, self **B.** 1. themselves 2. ourselves 3. yourselves **C.** myself, myself, yourself, themselves, himself

Page 57 **B.** 2 **C.** Answers will vary.